My First Dictionary

© 1993 Grandreams Limited

Published by
Grandreams Limited,
Jadwin House, 205/211 Kentish Town Road,
London, NW5 2JU.

Printed in Italy

AaBbCcDdEeFfGgHhIiJjKkLlMm

acorn
An acorn grows on an oak tree. Squirrels eat acorns.

aeroplane

An aeroplane is a machine that flies in the air.

alarm
An alarm is a loud noise. Alarm clocks wake you up.

ankle

An ankle is the joint between your foot and your leg. Your ankle lets you move your foot.

ant
An ant is a tiny insect.

antler

Antlers are the horns on a deer's head.

apple
Apples are a fruit that grows on a tree. Apples are nice to eat.
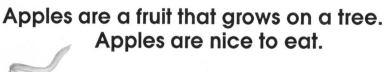

apron
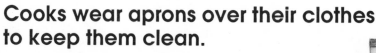
Cooks wear aprons over their clothes to keep them clean.

aquarium
An aquarium is a home for fish. There are many colourful fish in an aquarium.

arrow

You shoot an arrow from a bow. The American Indians hunted with a bow and arrow.

astronaut
An astronaut travels in space. A rocket can carry an astronaut to the moon.

axe

An axe is a tool used for chopping wood and to cut down trees.

ball   A ball is a round bouncy toy.

balloon   A balloon is filled with air. Balloons are bright and colourful.

bear   A bear is a strong, furry wild animal.

bell   A bell is something that makes a ringing sound.

blackberry   A blackberry is a small juicy fruit that grows on hedgerows.

bread   Bread is a food made from flour. It comes as a loaf.

bus   A bus carries lots of people from one place to another by road.

butcher   A butcher sells meat.

butter   Butter is made from milk. You spread butter on bread.

buttercup   A buttercup is a small yellow flower that grows in the countryside.

butterfly   A butterfly is an insect with pretty wings. A caterpillar turns into a butterfly.

button   A button is used to fasten clothes.

AaBbCcDdEeFfGgHhIiJjKkLlMm

cake
A cake is sweet and made from a batter. We have a special cake on our birthday.

camera
A camera is used to take pictures.

carrot
A carrot is a long orange vegetable. Rabbits like eating carrots.

castle
A castle is a big old building with tall towers where kings and queens used to live.

caterpillar
A caterpillar is a grub that changes into a moth or a butterfly.

cherry
A cherry is a small red fruit.

clown
A clown is an entertainer you see at the circus. Clowns make you laugh.

cone
Cones grow on fir trees. We use cones for Christmas decorations.

cow
A cow is a farm animal that gives you milk.

crab

A crab is a sea animal with a shell. Crabs are nice to eat.

crown
A crown is worn on the head. A king or a queen wears a crown.

cup

A cup is a small container with a handle. You drink from a cup.

daffodil A daffodil is a yellow flower that grows in the spring.

deer A deer is a wild animal that lives in the forest.

dice Dice have six sides, each with a different number of spots on. You use them when playing board games.

dinosaur A dinosaur is an animal that lived a long time ago.

dog A dog is an animal that barks. A dog is a family pet.

doll A doll is a toy that children dress up and play with.

dominoes Dominoes is a game. Dominoes are made of wood with spots on one side.

donkey A donkey is an animal with large ears. We can ride a donkey at the seaside.

dragon A dragon is an animal in fairy tales. They can be fierce or friendly.

dress A dress is a piece of clothing worn by girls and women.

drum A drum is a musical instrument. You can beat a rhythm on a drum with sticks.

duck A duck is a bird that swims in ponds and streams.

AaBbCcDdEeFfGgHhIiJjKkLIMm

eagle
An eagle is a large fierce bird. An eagle builds its nest high on a mountain top.

ear
The ear is the part of the body that we listen and hear with.

earth
The earth is the planet we live on.

eel
An eel is a snake-like fish that lives in the sea and rivers.

egg
An egg is laid by an animal or a bird. Eggs are good to eat.

elbow
The elbow is the joint in your arm between your wrist and your shoulder.

elephant
An elephant is a large animal with a trunk.

elf
An elf is a type of fairy in a story.

envelope
You send a letter or a card in an envelope.

eraser
An eraser is used to rub out pencil lines and marks.

eskimo
Eskimos live in very cold parts of the world.

eye
The eye is the part of the body that we see with.

falcon   A falcon is a bird of prey.

feather   A feather is part of the covering on a bird. Feathers can be very colourful.

fish   A fish is an animal that lives and breathes in water.

flag   A flag is a coloured cloth on a pole. Every country has its own flag.

football   A football is a special ball used in a football match.

frog   A frog is an animal that lives in or near water. Frogs hop from place to place.

gate   A gate is a door in a fence or a wall.

gloves   We wear gloves on our hands to keep them warm when the weather is cold.

goose   A goose is a bird with a long neck.

grape   Grapes are fruit that grow on vines. Grapes can be made into wine, or eaten dried as raisins.

grasshopper   A grasshopper is a green insect that hops.

guitar   A guitar is a musical instrument with strings.

hand   A hand is part of the body on the end of the arm. We have four fingers and one thumb on each hand.

hat    A hat is worn on the head to keep it warm.

heart   Your heart pumps blood around your body.

hedgehog    A hedgehog is an animal with lots of prickly spines on its back.

helicopter   A helicopter is a small aircraft. Helicopters can land on flat roofs.

helmet   You wear a helmet on your head to protect it from injury.

hen   A hen is a mother chicken. A hen lays eggs.

horn   A horn is an instrument that you blow.

horse   A horse is a large animal. We like to ride on a horse.

horseshoe   A horseshoe is a shoe a blacksmith puts on a horse's foot.

house   A house is a building that we live in.

hump   A hump is a large lump on an animal's back. Camels have humps.

ce Ice is frozen water. We make ice cubes to put in drinks.

ce cream  Ice cream is a sweet frozen dessert.

cicle An icicle is formed when dripping water freezes. Icicles hang on buildings and trees.

cing  Icing is a layer that we put on cakes. Icing is made of sugar and water.

gloo An igloo is a house made from blocks of snow. Eskimos live in igloos.

nk Ink is a coloured liquid used in pens for writing.

nsect  An insect is a tiny creature with six legs.

ris An iris is a tall flower used in flower arrangements.

ron An iron is used to press clothes smooth and remove creases.

sland An island is an area of land surrounded by water.

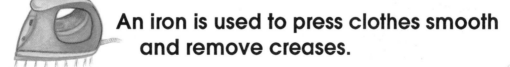

vy  Ivy is a plant that grows up walls and trees.

jacket   A jacket is a short coat. A jacket keeps you warm on a cold day.

jam   Jam is a very sweet food made from fruit. Jam is spread on bread.

jellyfish   A jellyfish is a round rubbery creature that swims in the sea.

jewellery   Jewellery is something we wear to decorate ourselves.

jigsaw   A jigsaw is a picture cut into pieces that you can fit back together.

jug   A jug is a container that we store or measure liquids in.

kangaroo   A kangaroo is a large animal that jumps. A baby kangaroo is carried in its mother's pouch.

key   A key is a piece of metal that turns a lock to open doors.

kite   A kite is a toy that you fly. You need a windy day to fly a kite.

kitten   A kitten is a baby cat. Kittens are very playful.

knife   A knife is a tool to cut things with.

koala   A koala is a small bear that lives in Australia.

label   A label is used on parcels and packages to say where they are going.

ladder   A ladder is something you climb up to reach a high place.

ladybird   A ladybird is an insect that can fly.

lamp   A lamp is a small light. We have a lamp to help us see at night.

leaf   A leaf is part of a plant or tree.

lemon   A lemon is a yellow fruit with a sharp taste. You make lemonade with lemons.

letter   A letter is a written message that you send to someone.

lips   Lips are a part of the mouth on our faces.

lizard   A lizard is a small animal. Lizards are reptiles.

lobster   A lobster is a sea animal with claws and a hard shell.

log   A log is a piece of wood cut from a tree. Logs are used on fires.

lorry   A lorry is a form of transport used to carry loads from place to place.

AaBbCcDdEeFfGgHhIiJjKkLlMm

map   A map is a drawing that shows us places on the earth's surface. Maps show us where to go.

match We strike a match when we want to make a fire.

meal   A meal is food that we sit down to eat at a table. Breakfast, lunch and dinner are meals.

meat  Meat is food from animals. Chops and steak are types of meat.

milk   Milk is a white drink we get from cows. Milk makes our bones and teeth strong.

mole  A mole is a small animal that digs tunnels under the ground.

monkey   A monkey is an animal that lives in trees. Monkeys are good climbers and swing through the trees.

moon The moon shines in the sky at night.

mountain   A mountain is a very high hill. Climbers like to climb mountains.

mouse  A mouse is a very small animal. You can keep a mouse as a pet.

mug   A mug is a tall cup without a saucer.

mushroom A mushroom is an edible fungus that grows quickly in wet places. Some types of mushroom are poisonous.

NnOoPpQqRrSsTtUuVvWwXxYyZz

nail   A nail is a thin piece of metal with a pointed end. You hammer nails into wood.

needle    A needle is a thin piece of metal with a hole in the end for putting thread through to sew with.

nest   A nest is a home made by birds. Birds lay their eggs in a nest.

nose   Your nose is the part of your face that you smell with.

number   Numbers are used for counting.

nut   A nut is food with a hard shell. Walnuts and almonds are nuts.

oar   You use oars to row a boat with. A rowing boat has two oars.

octopus   An octopus is an animal that has eight legs and lives in the sea.

onion   An onion is a vegetable with a bulb. Onions are used to flavour food.

orange   An orange is a delicious juicy fruit. We drink orange juice to get vitamin C.

otter   An otter is an animal that lives by river banks.

owl   An owl is a bird with large eyes. Owls sleep during the day and hunt at night.

paint   Paint is a coloured mixture that is used for painting pictures.

panda   A panda is a large black and white bear that eats bamboo shoots.

pear   A pear is a juicy, oval shaped fruit that grows on trees.

pen   A pen is a tool for writing in ink.

pig   A pig is a farm animal with a snout and bristly skin.

pigeon   A pigeon is a bird often seen in towns and parks.

pin   A pin is used to fasten material together.

potato   A potato is a vegetable that grows under the ground.

primrose   A primrose is a small yellow wild flower.

puppet   A puppet is a doll you move with strings.

puppy   A puppy is a baby dog.

purse   A purse is a small container to put your money in.

quail   A quail is a small bird with a short tail.

quarter  A quarter is one of four equal parts.

queen   A queen is a woman who rules a country.

quill A quill is a pointed feather used for writing long ago.

rabbit   A rabbit is an animal with long ears and a fluffy tail.

rake   A rake is a tool used in the garden. We rake up leaves.

ribbon   A ribbon is a colourful strip of material used to decorate things with.

ring A ring is a piece of jewellery that you wear on your finger.

robin   A robin is a small bird with a lovely red breast.

rose   A rose is a beautiful flower that grows in the garden. Roses have soft petals and a sweet smell.

rug   A rug is a small carpet.

ruler 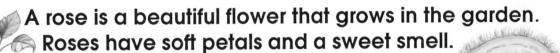 A ruler is a stick used for measuring.

sand castle   Children build sand castles at the seaside.

sandwich   A sandwich is two slices of bread with a filling between them.

scissors   Scissors are a tool we use for cutting up paper and material.

seal   A seal is an animal that lives in and near the sea. Seals eat fish.

shell   A shell is a covering for a sea creature. You can find empty shells on the beach.

socks   Socks are worn on your feet to keep them warm and comfortable.

spider   A spider is a small creature with eight legs. Spiders spin webs from very thin thread.

spoon   You use a spoon to eat with and to stir things.

squirrel   A squirrel is a wild animal with a big bushy tail.

star   A star is a bright light that shines in the sky at night.

strawberry   A strawberry is a sweet-tasting red fruit.

sun   The sun shines in the sky during the day. It gives us light and heat.

tadpole   A tadpole grows into a frog. Tadpoles are found in ponds.

teeth   Teeth are used for biting and chewing our food.

telephone   You use a telephone to talk to someone who is in a different place from you.

television    A television is a machine with moving pictures and sounds.

tent   A tent is a shelter made of tough cloth. We sleep in a tent when we go camping.

tomato   A tomato is a fruit that we eat with salad. Tomato ketchup is made from tomatoes.

train   A train takes people from one place to another. It runs along railway tracks.

tree    A tree is a large plant with a trunk and branches.

trumpet   A trumpet is a musical instrument that you blow.

tulip   A tulip is a flower with a long stem.

turkey   A turkey is a farmyard bird. Some people eat turkey at Christmas.

turtle    A turtle is an animal with a hard shell on its back. Turtles move very slowly.

AaBbCcDdEeFfGgHhIiJjKkLlMm

umbrella An umbrella is used to keep you dry in the rain.

unicorn A unicorn is a make believe animal that looks like a horse with a horn on its head.

uniform A uniform is a special set of clothing worn for a certain job. Soldiers wear a uniform.

vacuum A vacuum cleaner is used to suck up dirt and dust from a carpet.

van A van is a form of transport used for delivering things.

vase A vase is a container to arrange flowers in.

vegetable Vegetables are plants that we can eat.

vest A vest is part of our underclothes. We wear a vest on the top half of our bodies.

violet A violet is a small wild flower.

violin A violin is a string instrument. You play a violin with a bow.

volcano A volcano is a mountain containing hot ashes and burning rocks.

vulture A vulture is a bird of prey. It feeds on animal flesh.

waistcoat   A waistcoat is a small sleeveless jacket.

wasp   A wasp is an insect that has a sting in its tail.

watch   A watch is a small clock that you wear on your wrist. Watches tell us the time.

whale   A whale is the largest mammal that lives in the sea.

wheat   We use the grain from wheat to make flour.

wheelbarrow   A wheelbarrow is used to transport small loads.

whistle   A whistle is an instrument that makes a sharp sound when you blow it.

windmill   A windmill uses wind to make its sails go round.

window   A window is made of glass and it lets light into buildings.

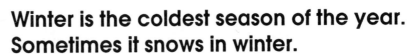

winter   Winter is the coldest season of the year. Sometimes it snows in winter.

witch   A witch is a wicked woman in stories who uses magic spells.

worm   A worm is a small creature with no legs. Birds like to eat worms.

XxYyZz

x-ray
An x-ray is a picture that shows the inside of your body. X-rays are used in hospitals.

xylophone

A xylophone is a musical instrument that you hit with a small hammer.

yacht
A yacht is a small boat used for racing.

yak

A yak is a big hairy animal with long horns.

yarn
Yarn is used for weaving and knitting.

year
Three hundred and sixty-five days make up one year.

yellow
Yellow is a bright colour.

yo-yo
A yo-yo is a toy. A yo-yo rolls down the string and spins up again.

zebra
A zebra is a horse-like animal with black and white stripes.
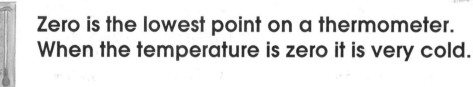

zero
Zero is the lowest point on a thermometer. When the temperature is zero it is very cold.

zip
A zip is a fastener for a coat. It has teeth which fit together.

zoo

A zoo is a special park where animals are kept. We visit the zoo to see the animals.